SNAKES SET I

ANACONDAS

Megan M. Gunderson
ABDO Publishing Company

visit us at
www.abdopublishing.com

Published by ABDO Publishing Company, 8000 West 78th Street, Edina, Minnesota 55439. Copyright © 2011 by Abdo Consulting Group, Inc. International copyrights reserved in all countries. No part of this book may be reproduced in any form without written permission from the publisher. The Checkerboard Library™ is a trademark and logo of ABDO Publishing Company.

Printed in the United States of America, North Mankato, Minnesota.
042010
092010

 PRINTED ON RECYCLED PAPER

Cover Photo: Getty Images
Interior Photos: Alamy p. 5; Getty Images pp. 11, 17, 21; Peter Arnold p. 9;
    Photo Researchers p. 19; Photolibrary pp. 6–7, 14–15

Editor: Heidi M.D. Elston
Art Direction & Cover Design: Neil Klinepier

Library of Congress Cataloging-in-Publication Data

Gunderson, Megan M., 1981-
 Anacondas / Megan M. Gunderson.
    p. cm. -- (Snakes)
 Includes index.
 ISBN 978-1-61613-432-7
 1. Anaconda--Juvenile literature. I. Title.
 QL666.O63G86 2011
 597.96'7--dc22
                                2010011003

CONTENTS

ANACONDAS

Anacondas are among the biggest snakes in the world! These water-loving animals are reptiles. So, they are vertebrates and are covered with scales.

Like other snakes, anacondas are cold-blooded. That means their surroundings affect their body temperature. Snakes warm up by lying in the sun. They seek out shelter to cool down.

Scientists recognize four species of anacondas. The green anaconda and the yellow anaconda are the most famous.

Very little is known about the other two species. The Beni anaconda is similar to the green anaconda. The DeSchauensee's anaconda shares features with the yellow anaconda. All anacondas belong to the family **Boidae**.

Green anacondas are also called great water boas.

Sizes

Green anacondas are the widest, heaviest snakes on Earth! They can weigh up to 450 pounds (205 kg). Their powerful, muscular bodies can grow quite long, too. Green anacondas usually measure 20 to 33 feet (6 to 10 m) in length.

Yellow anacondas are smaller than their green relatives. On average, they grow 7 to 10 feet (2 to 3 m) long. That's still an impressive size!

Female anacondas grow larger than males.

COLORS

The green anaconda is named for its coloring. Its back is dark or olive green. Big, black, oval-shaped spots mark its back. Spots with lighter centers line the green anaconda's sides. Its belly is yellow green. This reptile's coloring darkens with age.

As its name suggests, the yellow anaconda is yellow to tan in color. Pairs of black spots meet on its back. Crescent-shaped markings and smaller black spots mark its sides.

An anaconda's head has special coloring, too. The green anaconda has a stripe behind each eye. These stripes range in color from green to bright orange! The yellow anaconda has three dark stripes on its head. Together, these look like an arrow or a spear.

Black and orange stripes make some green anacondas look like they have horns!

WHERE THEY LIVE

Anacondas love spending time in water. So, they live in wet **habitats**. Green anacondas live near tropical rivers. They spend time in swamps, flooded forests, and slow-moving streams. Yellow anacondas are common in **savannas** that flood seasonally. They also live in swamps.

Green anacondas like to sun themselves on tree branches. Yet as they grow larger, they spend more of their time in water. The water helps support their massive weight. Yellow anacondas never reach those gigantic sizes. So, they spend more time on land and in trees than green anacondas do.

Green anacondas are never found far from water.
To dry off, they slither up into trees.

WHERE THEY ARE FOUND

Anacondas are native to South America. Yellow anacondas are found in Bolivia, Paraguay, and Uruguay. They also live in southwestern Brazil and northern Argentina.

Green anacondas have a huge range. It extends through Colombia, Venezuela, Guyana, Suriname, and French Guiana. These reptiles are found as far west as Peru and Ecuador. And, they live as far south as Brazil and Bolivia. These giant snakes also live on the island of Trinidad.

Pacific Ocean

SOUTH AMERICA

Atlantic Ocean

Detail Area

Where Anacondas Live

SENSES

An anaconda's eyes and nostrils are on top of its head. That way, the snake can see and breathe while it rests mostly underwater. The anaconda has a hard time seeing things that remain still. However, it is very good at spotting movement.

Like many animals, the anaconda uses its nostrils to smell. It also flicks out its forked tongue. This picks up scent particles in the air. Inside the mouth, the tongue enters the Jacobson's **organ**. This organ is in the roof of the mouth. It passes information to the snake's brain.

Since anacondas are snakes, they do not have **external** ears. That doesn't mean they can't hear. Instead, the bones in their lower jaws pick up vibrations. These flow through bones in their heads to their inner ears.

Snakes rely on a keen sense of smell to find food and mates.

DEFENSE

Anacondas stay safe by staying hidden. They blend in with their surroundings. This camouflage is an important defense against their enemies.

If an anaconda senses danger, it can simply slither away. If that isn't enough, the snake will attack. An anaconda has a mouth full of sharp teeth. The teeth release no **venom**, but their deep bite is still painful!

Adult anacondas are so large they have little to fear. Young green anacondas must watch out for foxes, lizards, and other natural predators. Crocodile-like caimans and larger green anacondas also pose a risk.

Humans are the anaconda's greatest enemy. They hunt anacondas for their skins. Humans also

When anacondas are still small, they make delicious snacks for caimans. But as these snakes grow, the caimans become the victims!

use green anacondas for medicines and meat. Some people even catch them for pets, but this is not recommended!

FOOD

A hungry anaconda will eat any animal it can swallow. It consumes fish, birds, mammals, and reptiles. The world's largest **rodent**, the capybara, is a common meal for green anacondas. These snakes even manage to swallow caimans.

The anaconda waits patiently at the water's edge for prey to wander by. Its coloring keeps it hidden. When an animal stops for a drink, the anaconda strikes out and grabs it.

This sneaky predator kills by constriction. It coils around its prey and squeezes until the animal can no longer breathe. The anaconda may also pull its prey underwater. A green anaconda can hold its breath for ten minutes while its prey drowns! Once the animal is dead, the snake swallows it headfirst.

Anacondas constrict animals as big as caimans. Then, they eat their prey whole!

BABIES

Mother anacondas often give birth in the water. The babies are born live, and they can swim right away. Yellow anacondas give birth to 4 to 20 babies at a time. Green anacondas have 4 to 80 babies. Larger, older anaconda mothers are likely to carry more babies at once.

At birth, yellow anacondas are about 18 inches (46 cm) long. Newborn green anacondas are more than 24 inches (61 cm) long. They will grow to nearly 10 feet (3 m) by age three!

All snakes are covered in scales connected by stretchy skin. They **shed** their outer layer for the first time soon after birth. Anacondas continue to do this as they grow throughout their lives. Soon, these growing anacondas will have babies of their own. Then, the life cycle begins again!

Baby anacondas start out small before growing into
the heaviest snakes on Earth!

GLOSSARY

Boidae (BOH-uh-dee) - the scientific name for the boa family. This family includes boa constrictors and anacondas.

external - of, relating to, or being on the outside.

habitat - a place where a living thing is naturally found.

organ - a part of an animal or a plant composed of several kinds of tissues. An organ performs a specific function. The heart, liver, gallbladder, and intestines are organs of an animal.

rodent - any of several related animals that have large front teeth for gnawing. Common rodents include mice, squirrels, and beavers.

savanna - a grassy plain with few or no trees.

shed - to cast off hair, feathers, skin, or other coverings or parts by a natural process.

venom - a poison produced by some animals and insects. It usually enters a victim through a bite or a sting.

WEB SITES

To learn more about anacondas, visit ABDO Publishing Company on the World Wide Web at **www.abdopublishing.com**. Web sites about anacondas are featured on our Book Links page. These links are routinely monitored and updated to provide the most current information available.

INDEX